At the Playground

Addition

Lisa Greathouse

Consultants

Chandra C. Prough, M.S.Ed.
National Board Certified
Newport-Mesa
  Unified School District

Jodene Smith, M.A.
ABC Unified School District

Publishing Credits

Dona Herweck Rice, *Editor-in-Chief*
Lee Aucoin, *Creative Director*
Chris McIntyre, M.A.Ed., *Editorial Director*
James Anderson, M.S.Ed., *Editor*
Aubrie Nielsen, M.S.Ed., *Associate Education Editor*
Neri Garcia, *Senior Designer*
Stephanie Reid, *Photo Editor*
Rachelle Cracchiolo, M.S.Ed., *Publisher*

Image Credits

cover Daniel Bendjy/iStockphoto; p.3 AlterYourReality/iStockphoto; p.4 Mark Bowden/ iStockphoto; p.5 Shutterstock; pp.6–7 (left) Paul Simcock/iStockphoto, (right) iStockphoto; p.8 (top) Craig Dingle/iStockphoto, (bottom) Photolibrary; p.9 Shutterstock; pp.10–11 (left) BigStock, (right) Monkey Business Images/Dreamstime; p.12–13 (left) Jennifer Hogan/Dreamstime, (right) Shutterstock; p.14 (left) Renee Keith/iStockphoto, (right) iofoto/iStockphoto; p.15 Stephanie Reid; pp.16–17 Shutterstock; p.18 (left) Nathan Gleave/iStockphoto, (right) Aldo Murillo/ iStockphoto; p.19 Shutterstock; p.20 (left) Shutterstock, (right) Francisco Romero/iStockphoto; p.21 Shutterstock; p. 22 (top) Shutterstock, (right) Bexcellent/Dreamstime; p.23 Shutterstock; p.24 monkeybusinessimages/iStockphoto; p.26 Shutterstock; p.28 Jani Bryson/iStockphoto

Teacher Created Materials

5301 Oceanus Drive
Huntington Beach, CA 92649-1030
http://www.tcmpub.com
ISBN 978-1-4333-3432-0

Table of Contents

We are at the playground.

There are so many things to **add**!

1 girl slides.
1 boy slides.

How many kids slide in **all**?

Add!

$$1 + 1 = 2$$

1 **plus** 1 **equals** 2.

2 kids slide in all.

He has 1 jump rope.
They have 2 jump
ropes.

How many jump ropes in all?

Add!

1 + 2 = 3

1 plus 2 equals 3.

There are 3 jump ropes in all.

1 girl plays basketball.
3 boys join her.

How many kids play basketball in all?

Add!

$$1 + 3 = 4$$

1 plus 3 equals 4.

4 kids play basketball.

He grabs 2 rings. There are 4 more rings.

How many rings in all? Add!

$$2 + 4 = 6$$

2 plus 4 equals 6.

There are 6 rings.

She crawls in 2 tunnels.

He crawls in 5 tunnels.

How many tunnels in all?

Add!

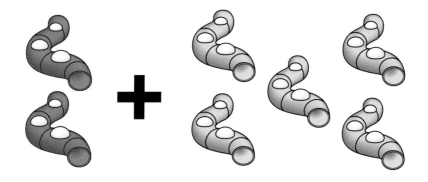

$$2 + 5 = 7$$

2 plus 5 equals 7.

There are 7 tunnels.

There are 3 red swings.

There are 2 blue swings.

How many swings in all?

Add!

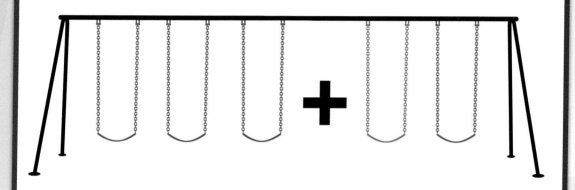

$$3 + 2 = 5$$

3 plus 2 equals 5.

There are 5 swings.

He climbs on 3 bars.
She climbs on 5 bars.

How many bars in all? Add!

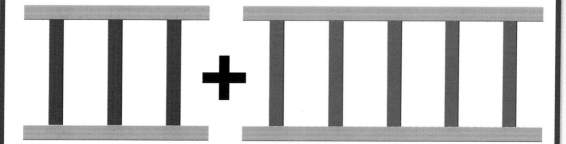

3 + 5 = 8

3 plus 5 equals 8.
There are 8 bars.

He plays with
5 shovels.

She plays with
4 pails.

How many toys in all? Add!

$$5 + 4 = 9$$

5 plus 4 equals 9.
There are 9 toys.

He rides on 1 car.
There are 4 more rides.

How many rides in all?

Add!

$$1 + 4 = 5$$

1 plus 4 equals 5.

There are 5 rides.

There are 4 green balls at the park.

There are also 2 red balls.

How many balls in all?

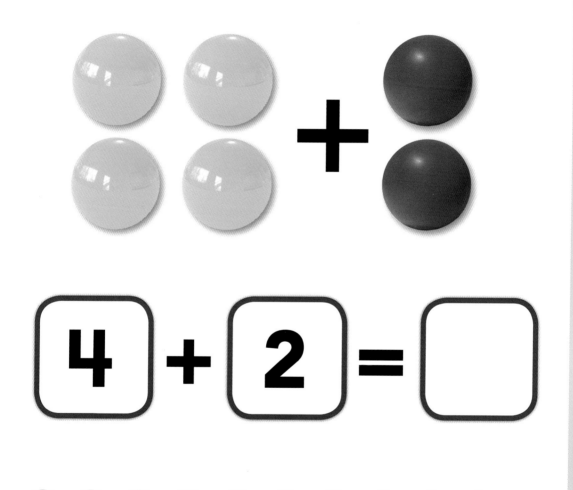

4 + 2 =

0 1 2 3 4 5 6 7 8 9 10

4 kids are playing tag.
6 more kids join them.

How many kids are playing tag in all?

How many jumping jacks can you do?

Materials
- ✓ number cards 0–5
- ✓ pencil
- ✓ paper

1 Pick a number card. Do that many jumping jacks.

2 Pick another card. Do that many jumping jacks.

3 Add. Write a number sentence to show how many jumping jacks you did in all.

(0) (1) (2) (3) (4) (5) (6) (7) (8) (9) (10)

Glossary

add—to find how many things there are in all

all—the whole amount

equals—has the same amount

plus—to add one amount to another amount

You Try It!

Pages 24–25:
4 + 2 = 6
There are 6 balls in all.

Pages 26–27:
4 + 6 = 10
10 kids are playing tag.

Solve the Problem
Answers will vary.